IMA

Ripley & Codnor

The Steam Mill Lane windmill in about 1910. It was used to grind corn and was demolished in about 1925.

IMAGES OF ENGLAND

Ripley & Codnor

David Buxton

NONSUCH

Mr G.A. Lynan making his final milk delivery round in the winter of 1958.

First published 1994
This new pocket edition 2005
Images unchanged from first edition

Nonsuch Publishing Limited
The Mill, Brimscombe Port,
Stroud, Gloucestershire, GL5 2QG
www.nonsuch-publishing.com

© David Buxton, 1994

The right of David Buxton to be identified as the Author of this work has been asserted in accordance with the Copyrights, Designs and Patents Act 1988.

All rights reserved. No part of this book may be reprinted or reproduced or utilised in any form or by any electronic, mechanical or other means, now known or hereafter invented, including photocopying and recording, or in any information storage or retrieval system, without the permission in writing from the Publishers.

British Library Cataloguing in Publication Data.
A catalogue record for this book is available from the British Library.

ISBN 1-84588-172-9

Typesetting and origination by Nonsuch Publishing Limited
Printed in Great Britain by Oaklands Book Services Limited

Contents

Robert and Myra Smith of Crossley Street on their wedding day in 1914.

Acknowledgements

I wish to thank everyone who has given advice, information and loaned photographs and other material for inclusion in this book. I have spent many happy hours sifting through old photographs and listening to stories of 'the old days' and I am very grateful for all the time these people have spent with me.

I would like to offer my special thanks to Wilf Marshall, Julie Potton, at Ripley Library, Monica Staley and Jim Melbourne who have been valuable sources of ideas and information, as well as pictures. In addition, thanks go to the following for allowing me to reproduce their photographs: Vera Alldread, Mr and Mrs Allsop, Mrs B. Ashley, Margaret Bilby, Mr and Mrs Bell, Mr B. Blount, Alice Blount, Bernard Bradley, Mrs I.Burgoyne, Mrs R.Buxton, Margaret Cheetham, George Eyre, Fowlers Music, Mr S. Fountain, Hallam, Whittle & Co, Mrs S. Hardstaff, Mrs D. Head, Ron Henshaw, Geraldine and Ken Holland, Muriel Honner, Mollie Hughes, John Hunt, Mrs N. Hunt, Minnie Illsley, Adrian Knifton, David Lamb, Mr and Mrs Loades, Frank Mancy, Mrs Matthews, Midland Railway Trust, Bill Nelson, G.C. Ogle Ltd, Olive Paradise, Irene Parker, Nora Rawson, Ellis and Alleyne Redfern, Mr and Mrs Revill, The Ripley and Heanor News, Ripley Hospital League of Friends, Ethel Rogerson, Miss S.Searson, John Shawcroft, Mrs Smedley, Keith Staley, Ernie Taylor, Don Waterall, Mrs D. Williams, Michael White.

There are three organisations in Ripley dedicated to the collection and preservation of old photographs and memorabilia of the area and all of them would be pleased to have the opportunity to see or hear about items that you may possess which relate to our local history. These are the Ripley Local History Society, the Ripley Heritage Centre, soon to open in Slack Lane, and Ripley Library. Do what you can to help them record and safeguard your heritage.

Introduction

This book is a nostalgic trip into the recent past of Ripley and Codnor. It does not try to be a history of the last hundred years but it does, through old photographs of people at work and play, old streets and shops, events and happenings, provide a sort of social history in visual form, for that period. Most of us enjoy looking at old photographs because they provide such a precise record of how things used to be. They show the clothes people wore, scenes of long lost buildings, special events of childhood, or our grandparents' childhood, and never fail to fascinate or evoke powerful memories.

Although a small number of the images used here may be familiar to people because they have appeared in newspaper articles or books over the years, most have never before appeared in print or indeed been seen outside the families or organisations that have preserved them. There are two well-known series of photographs in Ripley that have most often been drawn on in the past to illustrate articles. These are, first, the collection of the late Mr Len Wood, a large archive of photographs now deposited with the local library, and second, prints taken from the family negative collection of Mr Wilf Marshall, consisting of photographs taken by his father in the early years of the century. The Ripley area is very fortunate to have such an excellent record of its past preserved in this way and I have used photographs from both of these collections in this book. The combination here of formal portraits, postcard scenes, 'official photographs', company records and family snapshots make up, I hope, a fairly balanced look at life in Ripley and Codnor over the last hundred years or so.

Some of the biggest social changes that took place are typical of changes that occured over the whole country. These include changes in employment and industry that resulted from the effects of wars and the developing technology, the effects of the advent of the motor car which, among other things, allowed greater mobility and reduced dependence on local shops and facilities and then the arrival of television which signalled the end of home entertainment as it was known before the last war.

For a century and a half Ripley and Codnor were coalmining towns and any visitor in those days would be made aware of the fact immediately on arrival. The pits were obvious on all sides and mining activities dominated much of what most families did or saw during each day. Not only has all evidence of their existence vanished from view but two generations have grown up who never saw them or can remember the sights, the sounds or the smells. Other industries have declined and gone and even that major employer of Ripley men, the Butterley Company, needs only a fraction of its earlier workforce, whether it be to work iron or make bricks.

It is amazing to see in photographs from the 1900s to the 1950s, what a variety and choice of shops were available in Ripley. In the 1920s Church Street alone had seven provisions shops and Oxford Street had at least six butchers and all of them seemed to compete happily with each other and with the Co-op's own extensive facilities. Hardware shops, tinsmiths, drapers, house furnishers, jewellers that made watches, confectioners that sold their own sweets, cycle shops that made cycles to order, all found their niche and there was a baker in nearly every street! All of these excellent family-run concerns survived because everyone did all their shopping in town instead of in supermarkets and out of town shopping centres which we now drive to in our cars. What we have gained in convenience is, I fear, matched by what we have lost in personal service, the variety and choice of shops and hand-made goods.

Looking at these photographs one is struck by how much of leisure time was spent in home-made entertainment. Music was made by most families and some of them then entertained others with their skills. Carnivals occupied far more people in preparation and in participation than they do today. Social events that revolved around church and chapel activities were legion, as too were the number of active churches. Sport dominated free time for many and each church, works and school had football and cricket teams that competed in local leagues. Certainly these activities have not stopped, but its not like it was in the days of these pictures.

I hope that this collection of old photographs will bring back enjoyable memories for many and introduce new arrivals and a younger generation to the Ripley and Codnor that has only recently become history. One thing is for certain, there will be many a talking point in these pages!

David Buxton
October 1994

The old-established firm of Ellis-Fermor and Shephard (now Negus) on a staff day out to Mr and Mrs Shephard's bungalow at Sutton-on-Sea in 1947. Standing, left to right: June Goodwin, J.W. Henshaw, E. Burston. Mrs Thomson, Bernard Bradley. Seated: Barbara Finlay, W.W. Shephard, Mrs G. Shephard, Helen Armour.

One

Ripley Shops and Streets

Redfern's shop in Church Street in about 1910. This large shop sold a wide range of drapery goods and operated from 1871 until the 1930s when the firm sold the premises to Woolworths who remained there until a few years ago. Redfern's had one central cashier who dispensed change and receipts along overhead wires back to the customer at the counter. This device was always a source of interest to children.

Above: Numerous old family firms survive in Ripley but few can claim the longevity of Fowler's music shop in Oxford Street. Albert Fowler, its founder, opened his first music business in 1904 and the firm is still in family hands, three generations later. This was the original shop in Nottingham Road a building now occupied by Greenwich Post Office. He sold a range of musical instruments, gramophones and sheet music and taught piano and organ. He cycled near and far to reach his pupils and met his wife, a teacher, while giving lessons in Underwood.

Left: Albert Fowler was also a competent banjo and mandolin player and formed a seven-piece band.

Opposite above: Part of the Albert Fowler banjo band.

Opposite below: Fowler's music business moved to the present shop in Oxford Street in 1913. This photograph was taken in about 1920. He was the local agent for His Master's Voice and this picture shows not only the famous dog in the window but on the right-hand side are both cylinder and 78 rpm records. His daughter Alberta inherited the business in about 1948 and married Arthur Melbourne. The Melbourne family ran an off-licence business in Nottingham Road close to the Fowler's original shop. Their two sons, Jim and David, now run the much expanded business.

PIANOS · ALBERT FOWLER

The High Street, looking south from the end of Grosvenor Road, in about 1915. Shops from the right were: Fred Pickering, the butcher, Dilks, the hairdressers, (grandsons of the owner now have a similar business in Chapel Street), Miss Tomlinson, who sold pots (and had a reputation for eccentric behaviour!); then came an estate agent, followed by Logan's greengrocery and confectionery next to the Hippodrome.

The High Street looking towards the Market Place in the late 1940s. The clock on the wall on the right marks the position of Rowells' shop. The clock has now been moved to the other side of the High Street facing the end of Crossley Street.

This butcher's shop in the High Street was owned by the brother of Fred Pickering whose shop was seen in the top view of the High Street opposite. There were many butchers' shops in this area and in Oxford Street at the time. The postman in this picture of about 1920 is Mr Wharton and the butcher Sid Blount. This shop is now The Cob Stop.

GROCER
&
PROVISION DEALER
F.S. ALLSOP
CORN
&
FLOUR MERCHANT

Part of the interior of Allsop's shop in the High Street probably in the 1930s. This was a large and well-stocked establishment with a high reputation in the town. Mr F.S.Allsop was a shrewd businessman who traded in a variety of things as well as grocery. He owned stables in Slack Lane and in the early years of the century was said to be one of the largst dealers in horses in Derbyshire. He sold hay, straw and coal and supplied most of the local pits with pit ponies. This picture shows his son Fred with assistants Bertha and Edna.

Opposite above: The staff of Rowells' shop in the High Street in 1920. Rowells sold a wide range of drapery including, curtain materials, tapestries, upholstery and haberdashery materials but also finished garments such as coats, gloves, dresses and millinery. They also sold lino and coconut matting. Alleyne Redfern, who worked there in the late 1930s, remembers the chores of the youngest members of staff in the shop. Before starting work on the shopfloor each day it was her job to stoke up the boiler in the cellar, first raking out the ashes, then carrying the coke in buckets from the coal-hole under the pavement to the boiler at the back and lighting the fire. Rowells, who closed in 1979, also had shops at Heanor, Alfreton and Matlock. Boots now occupy these premises.

Opposite below: Allsop's grocery and provisions store in the High Street, c. 1910.

The staff at Allsop's shop in the High Street, *c.* 1905. The premises are now occupied by Fords.

F. S. ALLSOP, RIPLEY, DERBYSHIRE,
FOR HIGH-CLASS PIT PONIES.

Telegrams: FRED ALLSOP, RIPLEY, DERBYSHIRE — TELEPHONE 18

An advertisement for Allsop's pit ponies. The picture was taken in the Market Place facing the High Street shops and inns.

A trade show display of furniture by T. Greaves in the old dance-hall of the Hippodrome in 1948. Greaves' shop was opposite here on the corner of Oxford Street. They also had shops in Belper and Alfreton and a factory in Clay Cross. In 1952 the manager of the Ripley Branch, Herbert Hallam, with a colleague, Norman Whittle, set up their own furniture business in part of the old Hippodrome building across the road. These premises were extended to include their present shop in the High Street in the late 1970s. The firm is still in family hands today.

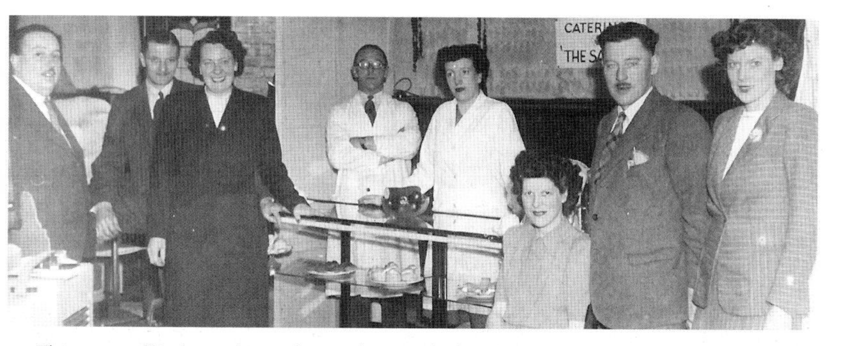

This group of Ripley tradespeople was photographed in the refreshments corner of the same furniture show seen above. The man on the left is Monty Castledine who became the first manager of the Hippodrome after it was sold by the Marshall family in 1946. On his left is Herbert Hallam who was the manager of Greaves at this time. Second and third from the right are Gladys and Phillip Hurse who had a television shop in the High Street in the 1950s and later in Oxford Street.

A view in about 1905 showing the spaciousness of the old Market Place and the Town Hall in its solitary splendour. Compare this with the new arrangement! The tree on the left is the Elm tree that is reputed to have stood there for 300 years and to have sheltered John Wesley on a preaching visit.

Albert Hawkins selling his own brand of sweets on Ripley market in the 1960s. His grandfather Wiliam Hawkins started the family business in the middle of the last century and the family had shops in Butterley Hill and Nottingham Road (see p.29). But it is for the special rock that Albert continued to make that the firm are best remembered. The rock was known as 'Tommy Dodd' and each stick had the image of a little man right through the middle. Albert had a small shop in Lowes Hill and made the rock in the 'boiling house' at the back. He was a well-known figure selling sweets on Ripley and Heanor markets and at Ripley Fair for fifty-six years.

Market Day in the early 1900s. Outside the White Lion on the left is a horse and brake belonging to Worthingtons of Jacksdale. Worthingtons ran a service to Ripley Market which later continued with buses. The two covered vans with chimneys on the High Street side of the stalls sold fish and chips.

Church Street in the early 1920s. The old Red Lion on the left had a thatched roof and offered a garage for its patrons although cars in Ripley at this time were not common. The Inn was badly damaged by a lorry in 1956 and, later, a new Red Lion was built and this finally closed in 1990. The shop on the right by the archway was Hunter's Tea Stores and along the street at this time were a large number of other food shops, all of which seemed to trade quite happily side by side. Among these were the Maypole, Home and Colonial, Standsbys, Melia's, London and Central Meat Stores and Blounts.

Church Street in the snow. This chilly-looking scene was taken in January 1979.

Church Street in the mid-1920s. The shop on the right had, a few years before, been a grocer's shop called Blounts. One Ripley resident remembers going there on Saturday mornings to pay the family grocery bill and getting a bag of broken biscuits to take home!

Ripley Town Hall in about 1920. Built in 1880 it replaced a more modest building that doubled as town and market hall.

This house stood on the corner of Chapel Street and Church Street where Brittain's shop and print works now stands. The old building had a stone over the door bearing the date 1675 which was preserved when the house was demolished and mounted inside the present building.

Brittain's Corner at the top of Chapel Street in the early years of the last century. Founded in 1874 by Mr G.C. Brittain, the shop was a popular toy shop and print works. The *Ripley and Heanor News* has been produced there for over one hundred years.

Right: Opposite Brittains was Arthur King's cycle shop, home of the 'King Cycle'. He began business in about 1880 in Derby Road, Hillocks and later moved to this shop in Chapel Street. A remarkable man to all accounts he made and repaired cycles of all kinds and was the first Ripley resident to own a motor car. His first journey in it to the annual garden party at Butterley Hall caused a sensation and people lined the streets to see him. He was also the first in Ripley to light his shop with incandescent light.

Below: Ripley Wesleyan Church in Chapel Street was just below Brittains. The chapel was the building on the left, the school room was in the middle, set back behind a garden, and the manse was on the right. The cars parked here are, from left to right, Riley, Standard Ten and Ford Prefect. The chapel buildings are gone and this site is now the Chapel Street car park.

The Ripley Co-operative Society began in a small shop on Butterley Hill in about 1860, founded by a group of workers from the Butterley Company. Like its counterparts all over the country the idea and the organisation grew rapidly and, by the turn of the twentieth century, the Ripley Society had a string of shops and services that dominated trade in the town. Co-operative Square was overshadowed by the Society's imposing head-office and central store building.

The Co-op menswear shop, situated in the main building, seen here in about 1910. This shop was situated under the blinds (fourth and fifth from left) in the picture above.

This is an early view of Co-op Square which must have been taken before 1909 because there is a gap beyond the Co-op building where the Electra Cinema was built in that year. The house on the right was the manse of the Ebenezer Chapel, which is now an estate agent's office.

When the trams came to Ripley, Co-op Square became the terminus. Here is a tram, arrived from Nottingham, waiting outside the Ebenezer Chapel in 1931.

The interior of the Co-op grocery in about 1910. Mr Searson was general manager here at this time and for many years after.

The Co-op foodstore in 1979. The Society had acquired the old Empire Cinema when it closed in 1956 and after some extensive conversions, including demolition and replacement of the frontage, it was reopened as the new foodhall. When the new Co-op superstore opened in Derby Road in 1981 this shop was vacated and became a carpet shop.

One of the Ripley Co-op delivery vans in about 1910. The man on the right is Tom Hill, head of the warehouse, and the driver is Kendall Scott Maïzey.

Grosvenor Road from Co-op Square in about 1922. The first house on the right was Miles, the dentist, the next was Watson's furniture shop, followed by a fish and chip shop with a billiards saloon above. Next came Leeson and Cope's estate agents before a pair of houses used as a maternity home. The site of the latter is now occupied by the library and Kwik Save. The Co-op wet fish shop was also in this road. The facing house at the far end, now part of the Market Place, was the house and surgery of Dr Feroze. In October each year a cattle market was held in the street with both ends closed off with cattle pens.

Just around the corner from the Co-op is Booth Street and the 'Workmens' Home'. In 1900 when work began to construct the tramline from Nottingham to Ripley and also to lay new sewers and water mains, there was an accommodation crisis for the large number of 'navvies' who were brought in to do the digging. John Marshall seized the opportunity and built a house for them and future itinerant workmen. This picture shows the opening ceremony in 1901. John Marshall is standing to the right of centre, with moustache and bowler hat, and to his left is the Ripley Medical Officer, Dr Boyle, whose surgery was in Cromford Road. On the extreme left is the architect, George Wesley Bird. On the opening day the public were allowed to look around for a penny and so many did so that £30 was collected and given to charity. The building as originally arranged could 'sleep' nearly 100 people: shared rooms were 4d or 6d and a private cubicle could be had for 8d. The building is now converted into flats and, in these more politically correct times, the name 'Workmens' Home' has been erased from the front.

The top of Nottingham Road in about 1922. The railing topped-wall on the left belonged to the Ebenezer Chapel. The shop in the middle belonged to George Hawkins and was an off-licence and brewery. His brother was Albert Hawkins, the sweet maker from Lowes Hill, so the shop always had a supply of home-made sweets for sale as well. The shop next door was Golding's newsagents, followed by Bowmer's, the bakers, and just around the corner was Hill's, the blacksmiths (see p.125). At the corner on the right was the Co-op grocery shop, part of this later became the Co-op shoe store and has now become the Athena fish restaurant. The next shop beyond this belonged to the Ripley Gas Company. In the distance on the right, was the entrance to Ripley Station.

The New Inn at the corner of New Street and Oxford Street in the early 1900s. Priestley's music and electrical shop has occupied this building since about 1910.

The Ripley Co-op retained stables and horse-drawn milk floats for deliveries until the 1960s. This photograph shows milkman Chris Hickling in the stable-yard in Crossley Street in 1964.

A view of Oxford Street in the 1890s. The lamp on the wall on the left may show the position of the old Angel Inn.

The Oxford Street shops of John Marshall in about 1905. He first came to Ripley from Clay Cross in 1888 as a young watchmaker and with capital of £20. He opened his first shop, selling watches and jewellery, nearer to the bottom end of Oxford Street, using a converted house window to display his stock. He moved to these premises in 1900 adding a hardware shop to the business. John Marshall stands with his wife, Sarah, and daughter Edith while son Jack looks after the hardware. His business had grown fast. He had by this time also built the 'Workmens' Home' in 1901. Three years later he opened the Ripley Zoo and, in 1913, the Hippodrome.

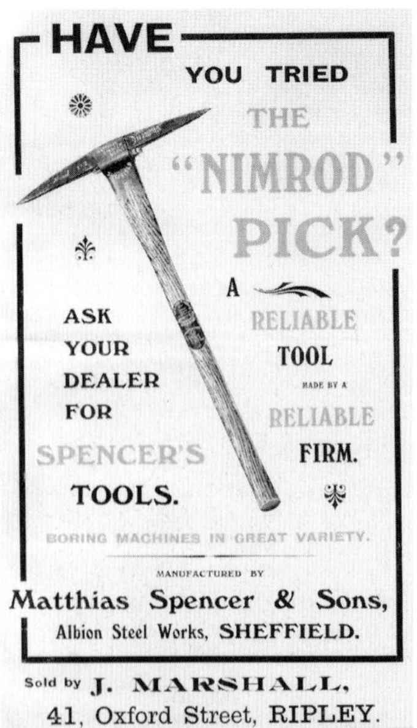

Above: Another Marshall shop. Sarah Marshall ran a confectionery shop adjacent to the family's other two shops. This photograph was taken at about the same time, in 1910, as the one opposite and this arrangement of the pictures mimics their positions in the street. The zoo entrance was through the archway between them. There were refreshment rooms and for the sum of 2d cyclists could leave their bikes here in safe keeping while they shopped.

Left: Handbill advertising miners' tools for sale. Miners were expected to buy their own tools before the days of the National Coal Board.

Jack Marshall stands at the door of the 'Wedding Ring King' in about 1910. From 1928 his brother Wilf Marshall took over the running of the hardware business and combined the three family shops into one. He sold a wide range of tools, hardware and paints. The business was eventually sold in 1960 when he retired. The newsagent's shop, visible on the right, belonged to Miss Helling.

This advertisement for Marshall's tools is one of a series of coloured lantern slides that were used to advertise local businesses during the intervals at the Hippodrome in the early 1930s.

Above: Oxford Street in the snow in about 1910. The view looks towards the High Street.

Left: Mr Helling was a tinsmith and ironmonger in Oxford Street up to about the time of World War I. When he retired the shop was taken over by his apprentice, Mr Daniel, and he moved in to live with his sister next door who ran the newsagents shop.

Opposite: Helling's stationery and newsagents shop in Oxford Street in about 1922. Standing in the doorway is Sabina Pickard (later Johnson) who started work in the shop at the age of thirteen years and continued to work there for most of her life, taking over the business from the Hellings in about 1938. Mr and Mrs Johnson bought this and the neighbouring shop in about 1958 and their daughter Margaret has continued to run the now expanded shop to the present day.

EST BEST
TURES PICTURES
BEST BEST
PICTURES PICTURES
PATTERN SHOP
HELLING
STATIONER & NEWSAGENT

Above: Oxford Street in about 1910. The trees on the left grew in the Jordan's garden where at least one local lad recalls scrumping apples. Shops on the right included those of Hellings and Marshalls and, further down on the right, was Mr William Lacy's newspaper shop. He was a popular figure and gave rides to children in his pony and trap as he delivered the papers which were collected from Butterley Station each morning. He had a wooden leg and was known to disrespectful local children as 'Pegleg Lacey'.

Left: The house and studio in Oxford Street of Randolph Nield, the Ripley photographer, in about 1910. These buildings, now demolished, were on the north side of the street near the bottom end. This picture, taken not by him but by John Marshall, records the day that his chimney was struck by lightning.

Above: This row of houses on the south side of Oxford Street, near the bottom end, were demolished in 1977 and are seen here shortly before that time. The second house on the left, after the shop, was owned by John Marshall when he first arrived in Ripley in 1888 and the enlarged window was fitted by him as a shop window.

Right: Percy Wilkinson and his shop in Oxford Street in the 1960s. His shop, now demolished, stood opposite Fowler's music shop and was in two parts with a door at each end. At one end he sold herbal products and at the other, sweets, ice-cream and candyfloss.

JOIN THE MINERS . . . but don't go down the mine Daddy without your

Procea bread

ONCE TASTED—NEVER WASTED!

Procea Products Ltd., Procea House, Dean Street, London, W.1.

F. E. & D. W.

MOSS

Bakers and Confectioners

47 OXFORD ST., RIPLEY

DERBYSHIRE

for High Class

BREAD AND CONFECTIONERY

Birthday, Wedding and Christening Cakes a Speciality.

There has been a bakery at 47 Oxford Street for close on 100 years. Starting as Kemp's around the turn of the century it was run by the Moss brothers from the 1940s to the 1980s. This advertisement appeared in a guide to Ripley, produced in 1949.

This was the shop front of Moss's bakery when it changed hands in about 1984. The present owners, Mr and Mrs Bell, have retained the old name, but fitted a new frontage.

Right: John White was the founder of White's, the jewellers, now in Oxford Street. He began with a shop in Marehay in 1884 trading as a jeweller, watchmaker and optician. In 1889 he moved to Station Road and in 1900 moved again, this time to a custom built shop in Nottingham Road. He widened his business to include musical items such as gramophones, pianos and wireless and also tobacco and fancy goods. This shop is now the House of Tom Peel.

Below: His wife and later his sons ran the business after his death in 1914. By 1969 the firm was once again specialising in jewellery alone and in 1974 moved to its present position in Oxford Street. This blotter dates from the time in Nottingham Road and was one of a series of complimentary items given to customers in the 1930s.

BLOTTER

Established 1884 Phone 46

JOHN WHITE & SONS

DEPARTMENTS

Watchmaking Jewellery and Silversmiths .	Pianos, Gramophones and Wireless "PYE" SERVICE AGENTS	Wholesale & Retail Tobacco and Fancy Goods

36-38 NOTTINGHAM ROAD

RIPLEY (Derbys.)

Closed and awaiting the bulldozer. These shops in Oxford Street, due for demolition in 1981, were replaced by new shops including a new branch for the TSB.

Demolition in Oxford Street. These shops in the middle of the north side of the street came down in 1981.

A smart 'Chevrolette' delivery van of Beach and Loades bakery in 1925. The firm at this time had two motorised vans and a horse-drawn one. The partnership of Herbert Loades and his brother-in-law Henry Beach was set up in 1918 when they bought Kay's bakery, close to the end of Dannah Street, in Nottingham Road. Both ex-miners, they successfully took up baking and confectionery and the firm grew. Henry Beach died of typhoid in 1922 and his nephew Walter joined the firm as partner. Walter is on the right in this photograph with van driver, Fred Archer. Walter left the firm in 1937 and it became H. Loades and Son, continuing until the 1970s, when it became part of Blanchards. In 1926 Herbert also joined his brother Albert in a business partnership to set up a match factory in Steam Mill Lane. The enterprise appears to have been largely the idea of Albert, with Herbert providing some of the financial and organisational support (see p.116).

Above: Beach and Loades' shop in Nottingham Road in the 1920s. Standing in front of the shop are Ethel Loades and her son Thomas.

Left: The interior of Beach and Loades' bakehouse in about 1932. The large bins in the foreground contained sugar and flour. In the picture, from left to right are: Thomas Loades, Walter Beach, Dennis Fox and Ron Bayliss.

Opposite above: Nottingham Road, Greenwich in about 1905.

Opposite below: A tram and a group of ladies in cloche hats in Nottingham Road in about 1925. The road on the right is Eastfield Road. The fields on the left now accommodate houses and the Codnor Park Industrial Estate.

Greenwich, Ripley.

A peaceful day on Butterley Hill, around the beginning of the last century.

Butterley Hill in 1914. The building on the left was the mineral water factory of Burrows and Sturgess which later became a cosmetics factory. The mineral water was delivered to shops in the area by Mr Rankin and Mr Collins in a horse-drawn cart.

The Roundhouse on Butterley Hill was demolished in about 1980. The new Woodlands Nursing Home is now on this site.

Argyll Road in about 1912. The road at this time was a private one with wooden posts half way down to prevent traffic passing through.

All the houses in this picture of Hammersmith taken in about 1910 survive today. The terrace on the left was once known as 'Poker Row'. The cottages were owned by the Butterley Company and when the rent collector called, so the story goes, the tenant at the first house would bang the wall with a poker to warn the next house of his arrival and so the alarm was passed on down the street. The factory visible at the end of the street was a wire factory which later became a spring works.

Shops built as branches of the Ripley Co-op can still be seen all over the town and its outskirts. They are recognisable by their size and design but none of them remain as Co-op shops. This one was the Hillocks Branch in Derby Road. Mr Arthur Lamb was the manager here during World War II. He started with the Co-op as an errand boy in 1908 for six shillings a week.

Cromford Road seen from the corner of Victoria Road, also known as Ogle's Corner, in about 1920.

The terrace known as Horse and Jockey Row after the inn at end of the row. All these houses were demolished soon after this photograph was taken in 1967. Pasteur Avenue now leads off to the right were they stood.

This large house in Derby Road was the old surgery of Dr Thompson, which was demolished in 1980 for the building of the new Co-op Superstore.

Derby Road in the 1930s.

Two

Road and Rail

Learning to drive in 1920. Will Mander of Mander's Garage in Derby Road taught Miss Wallace to drive this de Dion car and had postcards made of the picture, perhaps to promote his cars. From the back of this photograph we learn that it had an 8 H.P. engine, an accumulator, one steel-studded Dion skid tyre, a two-seated body (but seats three), three lamps and expanding clutch gears (two speeds and reverse). The wheel spokes were made of wood and the price was £40.

Ripley Station in about 1910.

Part of Ripley Station buildings in 1963 after closure of the station. Clower's the builders used the buildings as offices until the 1970s after which they were demolished.

A clear view of the Ripley Station taken on a day for the train 'buffs'. A 'special' train enters the station from Derby in 1956.

Above: A train entering Ripley Station from Derby in about 1929.

Left: When Clower's builders demolished the station at Ripley this decorative Midland Railway 'keystone' was saved and is now preserved at the Midland Railway Centre.

The station master stands for a photograph on the platform at Crosshill Station, Codnor in the 1920s. One wonders whose job it was to maintain his well-stocked station garden.

A Butterley Company Railway Loco (no.9) built in 1917 and still in use many years later after a refit. The driver is Tom Birkin, jnr and the photograph is probably from the 1930s. Possibly because Butterley locos were only used by the company and on their own track they had a distinctly 'utilitarian' design and livery compared to main-line company trains.

Butterley Station in 1955. Although the station was close to the Butterley works it was not their responsibility but part of the Midland Railway. It was opened in 1875 and handled a good deal of freight traffic, particularly coal and iron from Butterleys. Passenger services also supplied the needs of local people and employees at the works.

The 'new' Butterley Station at the Midland Railway Centre in about 1980. After the closure of the original station and line a group of railway enthusiasts began to investigate the possibility of using the site, and what was left of track and other memorabilia, for exhibiting preserved railway effects including locos and rolling stock. This photograph shows what appears to be the station buildings intact but is in fact Whitwell Station, carefully dismantled and transferred to Butterley, and now in use as a ticket office for the newly formed Midland Railway Centre.

One of the early open days and 'steaming events' in about 1979 at the Midland Railway Centre with visitors exploring a range of exhibits on view for the day.

The Railway Bridge across Butterley Reservoir in about 1910 and before the sides of the structure were built up and filled in. The reservoir was formed to act as a head of water for the Cromford Canal. Butterley works are visible beyond the bridge. Some Ripley residents remember skating on the ice here during hard winters in the early part of the last century.

The Derby to Ripley railway line once crossed the Derby Road at Marehay. This photograph was taken as the last crossing was made before the line was abandoned in 1963. The Marehay Garage is visible on the left.

This photograph of the Marehay Garage was taken in 1931. That year Bill Hunt left his job at Blake's blacksmiths in Malthouse Yard, Ripley and borrowed £100 from his sister to buy the premises at Marehay. Bill is seen in the picture with his first apprentice in front of the converted barn that was the workshop.

Marehay Garage in about 1945. The garage was an agent for Anglo-American petrol, later Esso, and is one of the oldest agents for the brand in the country. The original barn workshop is still in use at the garage today but now as the company offices. The people on the forecourt are, from left to right: George Wheatley (employed for 50 years), Mr Fox, Bill Hunt, George Wheatley, snr and, in front of the garage's Ford van, Wilfred Hunt. The car on the right is Bill Hunt's Vauxhall.

The last of the trolley buses in Ripley, photographed in Beighton Street in May 1953.

Olive Mander riding a bicycle in the yard of her father's garage in Derby Road in about 1930. Olive Paradise, as she now is, can still be found working at the garage that her family founded in about 1920. Her grandfather bought Saxton's farmhouse, (in this picture), in about 1903 and operated here as a wheelwright. Mander's became the first garage in the Ripley area. Like many smiths and wheelwrights at the time the family had begun by mending cars and bicycles and then started selling them and the petrol for them. Her father, Will, was the first to stock petrol in the town, which he collected when it was needed from Kennings at Clay Cross – two six gallon cans at a time.

Mander's Garage in the 1950s. By this time the farmhouse had been replaced by a new house for the family and new pumps installed on the forecourt – exactly where the old farm gateposts had been. The pump on the left was a Theo Multiple which could dispense any one of six types of petrol and was unusual for its time. Drivers could choose between Shell, BP, National Benzole, Cleveland Discol or Power. When the old house was taken down in 1938 the bricks were used to build air-raid shelters but the tiles were kept until 1959 and used to roof the new garage building which is still in use.

If you lived in Heage or Belper in the 1920s this is the bus you might have caught to Ripley market. The bus was a Ford but the coachwork was built by Will Mander and his father. There were regular runs between the towns on market day (Saturday), with a special late run back to Belper leaving Ripley at 11.00pm!

The first tram arrives at Ripley terminus from Nottingham in 1913. Not surprisingly a large crowd turned out to watch, it had long been anticipated. The building on the right, next to the Co-op building, is the manse of the Ebenezer Chapel. The journey to Nottingham by tram took two hours!

Three ages of the train side by side at an open day at the Midland Railway Centre in about 1980.

Three

Ripley Zoo

In 1908 Ripley acquired a most unlikely addition to its attractions. Local businessman and entrepreneur John Marshall opened his zoological gardens. Not one to do things by halves, Mr Marshall included a display of wild animals, a museum, a waxworks exhibition, a tea room and a children's roundabout and, what's more, assembled it all right in the centre of town in Oxford Street. John Marshall is seen here by the entrance to the museum with his daughter Edith, and his son Jack; both are holding animals on their laps. The crocodile in the foreground was not a live exhibit!

The entrance to the zoo was in Oxford Street through the archway between Mrs Marshall's sweet shop (left) and John Marshall's jewellery shop (now Cellar 5). The entrance was surrounded by signs, stuffed animals and photographs of the exhibits taken by the proprietor. Visitors entered the passageway to the sounds of brass band music played on a gramophone near the door. The boy in the uniform is Richard Marshall, who later managed the Hippodrome Cinema, and he stands here in the entrance with his sister Mabel. The little boy on the left is Charlie Cutts who later became a popular singer in local operatic society events.

Above: A group of visitors outside the monkey house in about 1910. Several of these children were to become tradespeople in the town; Wilfred Parkin (front row, centre) and his brother Jack (one of the boys in caps on the back row) ran an outfitters business. Above the monkey house can be seen one of three viewing platforms. The one at house-roof level gave an unusual chance to see across the rooftops of Ripley.

Right: Jack Marshall, the eldest son, was the animal trainer and is said to have had great skill in handling the animals.

Above: John and Sarah Marshall photographed in the home 'studio' (probably on the flat roof) before one of the painted backcloths in about 1920. John Marshall was a man who could, and often did, turn his hand to almost anything. He was never daunted by a lack of experience! He was an excellent photographer and recorded many family and town events. He took this picture of himself using an early type of delayed exposure device. He recorded Ripley on cine-film in the 1920s. It is not known what gave him the idea of opening a zoo because as far as anyone knows he had not had any previous experience of keeping or displaying animals.

Left: The squirrel house and gardens at the zoo.

Some more of the zoo roof gardens including one platform amongst the chimneys! Some of the Marshall family are sitting on a bench at the lower level.

The aviaries held a variety of foreign and British birds. The clock at the top of the cage was made by John Marshall and was unusual for its wooden mechanism. The mechanism eventually rotted away but the face was preserved and is still in the possession of his surviving son.

A children's roundabout on one of the roof gardens.

Above: Humphrey Marshall with two dogs, a parrot and a cockatoo. The zoo did not survive the First World War, fears of shortages of food for the animals led to its closure in 1915. Most of the remaining animals were sent to Regent's Park, London or Belle Vue in Manchester although some, like these birds, were kept as family pets.

Right: The Marshalls enjoying a snowball fight on the roof.

Jack Marshall in the snow-training a sealion to do tricks. Behind him is the old elm tree that stood in the Market Place, reputedly, for 300 years. By about the turn of the century it was dead but it was allowed to remain in its position for some years (see photograph on p.18). When it was eventually removed, the Marshalls acquired it and displayed it in the zoo garden.

Above: This photograph and the one below show the whole Marshall family. This one taken in about 1910 on the roof overlooking Oxford Street shows the family up to that time. From the left: Jack, Harold, John, Richard, Sarah, Humphrey (on his mother's lap), Mabel and Edith. There is what appears to be an elephant's foot on the right of the picture.

Right: This must have been taken in about 1913 because it shows Thomas, in a sailor suit, and baby Wilfred, the surviving member of this generation of Marshalls. They are sitting outside the reptile house which contained snakes and a variety of small reptiles.

Another busy day at the zoo. One wonders what the neighbours felt about the loss of privacy in their homes when these platforms were built for the public to stand and peer from! Just one curious aspect of the Ripley zoo is how so much was accommodated in the relatively small space available between the houses and shops in such a central position in the town. Probably the largest animal that was kept at the zoo was a bear. When it became sick with pneumonia it was put down by the pork butcher, Mr Hogg, from across the road in Oxford Street. He also skinned it and the hide was cured and used as a rug on the landing in the Marshalls' house.

The view across Oxford Street to the Co-op buildings from the top platform, in about 1910.

This is the view from the same platform but looking the other way, over the children's roundabout towards Crossley Street. The cost of entry to the zoo was 2d for adults and 1d for children. Crowds of children would often come for the whole day for their penny, arriving with a bread and jam sandwich and a bottle of water!

Above: One of John Marshall's efforts to record his family for posterity. Here are four generations of his wife Sarah's family (Walters). Sitting here on the roof garden with her are, from the left, her grandfather, her father and her son Jack.

Left: As well as the animals at the zoo there was also a waxworks exhibition. It was claimed that this grotesque figure, called Bifiz, was modelled from a real 'individual'. According to the display plate Bifiz was, 'Born in San Fransisco of an Indian mother and a Burmese father. Her body is hermaphrodite. Now living in South India'.

Opposite: Another of the exhibits from the waxworks that must have been a source of nightmares for more than a few Ripley children at the time! This one was described as a Chinese warrior's armour. The wall behind the figures is decorated with reptile skins.

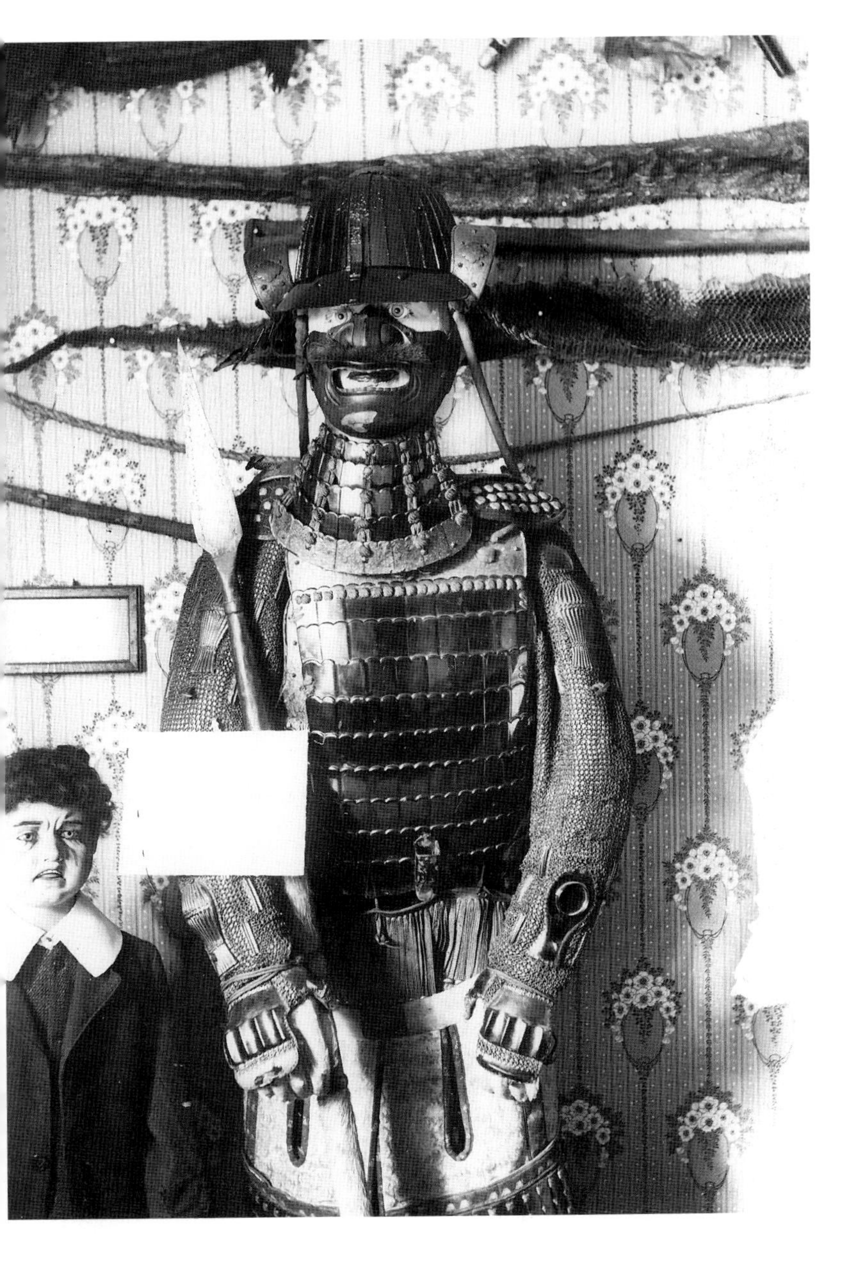

As we leave the amazing displays at Ripley zoo gardens behind and venture back outside into Oxford Street, we look back up the passageway to the zoo entrance where Edith Marshall waits to greet the next visitors.

Four

Codnor Shops and Streets

Codnor Market Place in the early years of the twentieth century. The Severn's shops were built later on the right from bricks salvaged after the demolition of the steam mill in Steam Mill Lane, Ripley. The cottages on the left have now gone.

Mr and Mrs White, landlord and landlady of the Glasshouse Inn in about 1900. Mr White was related to the Bowker family of Greenwich Farm, Hillocks, Ripley.

Codnor Post Office and general store in about 1905. Like many small town post offices of the time the shop also stocked a wide range of groceries and other goods. Included in the stock here were tinned and dried foods, bacon and dairy products. A plate on the wall advertises the famous Mazawattee Indian tea.

Crosshill Schools in about 1910.

Glasshouse Hill in about 1898. The little boy, who is apparently quite safe standing in the middle of the road, is George Large who lived in this road. He later became a market gardener in Nottingham Road, Ripley.

The parish church in Crosshill in about 1905.

Acorn Farm at Wood Lincoln, Nottingham Road, Codnor, home of the Brown family. Albert Hawkins, the sweet-maker from Lowes Hill, Ripley was a son-in-law to the family and is seen here with his children Albert and Vera, feeding the chickens, in about 1930.

Mill Lane, looking up from the Market Place, in about 1914.

A Codnor carnival parade to celebrate the Coronation in 1937. The photograph was taken by Bert Hurst, the pharmacist, from the window of his chemists shop on the corner of Mill Lane. Pulling a model of the Queen Mary, in hastily borrowed sailor suits, are George Eyre and Harry Joyce followed by Peter Kemp who is dressed as a Dutchman. Bert Hurst later moved his business to Ripley.

The Jessop Arms in Jessop Street in about 1900.

Wright Street, looking up from Jessop Street towards Mill Lane in about 1900.

Mrs Ellen Hutchinson of Codnor. Her grandson Enoch founded the Ripley Scouts and his family are still involved in the scouting movement.

Five

Sports and Leisure

Ripley Tennis Club in the late 1920s. The player on the left is Mr Statham, father of Ron Statham a nationally known Ripley player of his day who played at Wimbledon. The lady is probably Mrs Muriel Honner. The club was reformed in 1947 after a gap of several years and still occupies the same site in Heage Road today. At the time of this photograph there was no clubhouse and a tent was used instead.

The 'Fiddler Shaws'. The Shaw family farmed a small-holding at the top of Peasehill but were also a popular musical troupe. They travelled the area playing concerts at dances and other social events, often walking long distances to play. This photograph taken in about 1882 shows Mr Shaw on the left with his daughter, little Harriet, on the triangle, son John on second fiddle, Tom playing the harp and a third son, whose name we do not know, on flute. Mr Shaw also worked in the Butterley Company bridge yard. When Harriet was a little older she sold farm milk around Ripley from pails carried on a yoke.

Crossley Park soon after its opening in 1935. It was created on land given to the town by James Crossley in 1901.

Butterley boilersmith Arthur Staley and his wife pose with great style for this studio picture whilst on holiday at Skegness in 1924. Skegness was a popular seaside resort for Ripley people. Arthur came from London to work in the Ripley pits as a smith after being engaged by Butterleys on the St Pancras station construction.

Above: The wrestler on the right in this studio portrait is Percy Illsley. He was Midlands Featherweight Wrestling Champion in the 1920s and is seen here with some of his trophies and wrestling colleague Alf Elliott. Percy was born in Ripley in 1893 and took up wrestling whilst in the Ripley Church Lads' Brigade. He began work as a baker at Kemp's Bakery (now Moss's) and later worked as a miner at Denby Hall Colliery. He was a successful amateur wrestler for many years and remained a keen athlete and fitness expert for much of his life. He gave athletic and acrobatic displays locally until he was well into his fifties. He died in 1977 aged 84 years. His wife Minnie, continued to live in Ripley.

Left: Percy Illsley and athletic friends giving an acrobatic display at Monsal Dale in the 1920s.

John Marshall (standing) was also a local fitness expert. He is seen here with Percy Illsley in a 'classical' pose taken for a book of 'Physical Culture' which was put together by the former for publication in the 1920s. John Marshall was also a professional stunt man and after an initial career with the Ripley Co-op emigrated to the United States and made a living there in the film industry. Apparently one of his favourite stunts was to perform handstands on the tops of skyscrapers.

The start of a long career in the motor business. Olive Mander takes the driving seat of her father's Sunbeam outside the family farmhouse behind the garage in Derby Road in 1927.

AC 1422

Ripley United Silver Prize Band won the Daily Sketch Cup and the Junior Championships of the British Empire at Crystal Palace in 1930. The band assembled here in the garden of Josiah Brown in Shirley Road consisted of; back row, left to right: Job Saint, Walter Saint, Ernie Lamb, Maurice Wileman, Joe Cowley, Joe Holmes, Lol Cuttel, Tom Saint. Middle row: George Battison, Bill North, Jim Wall, Tom Curzon, Tom Crossley, Harry (Jock) Townsley, Charlie Bailey, Fred Cuttel, Jim Bratby, Jack York. Front row: Bill Careless, Oliver (Taffy) Williams, Gren Hawkins, Harry Armstrong (Secretary), W.J. Saint (Bandmaster), Alf Curzon, Fred (Final Freddie) Palmer, Ralph East.

Off to Matlock for the day. A group of Ripley ladies board a charabanc by the bank at the end of Grosvenor Road in about 1912. The vehicle was one of Raven's Bluebird Charabancs.

The Butterly Glee Club in about 1918. The group was photographed in Jordan's garden in Oxford Street, an area now occupied by shops. In the background can be seen part of the shop which belonged to W.A. Daniel, tinsmith, which now forms the right hand part of Johnson's the newsagents.

The Electra Theatre was Ripley's first purpose-built cinema and theatre. It replaced Wood's shoeing forge (below) on the site facing up Church Street in Co-op Square. It opened in 1909 and showed a regular programme of films. This was a great growth period for the cinema in Britain and one that saw a rapid increase in the number of new theatres in other towns nearby. By 1911 the Electra was already deemed to be too small to accommodate the demand in Ripley and it was replaced by larger and grander building called the Empire.

The forge that predated the Electra Cinema had earlier been a Dissenter's Chapel.

Above: The Ripley Empire was built on land leased from the Ripley Co-operative Society and adjacent to the main Co-op buildings. The theatre had a large stage and could seat over 600 people. Norman Gray who had been the manager of the Electra continued as manager of the Empire. In the 1930s Albert Hall was manager. The Empire closed in 1956. The cinema frontage was demolished in 1959 and the building was incorporated into the main Co-op buildings.

Right: A scene from the Ripley Co-operative Operatic Society's production of *Tom Jones* in 1948.

Some of the ladies who made ammunition boxes during World War I at Gee's factory in Malthouse Yard, off Church Street, also enjoyed a game of football. The team was apparently a successful one, judging by the trophy held by the captain. Mr Gee started this small factory at the beginning of the war with a loan of £100. The business grew from these small beginnings to become the building company of Gee, Walker Slater. In the picture are: back row, left to right: J. Ellis, G. Holmes, F. Brown, M. Holmes, J. Gee. Middle row, E. Taylor, E. Davenport, D. Hall. Front row: P. Ottewell, R. Hunt, E. Bassett, A. Brown, M. Daley.

The Snowflake Minstrels troupe line up outside the Baptist Assembly Hall in Church Street before a concert party in the 1930s. Most of the performers are known; back row, left to right: -?-, -?-, Matt Brough, A. Doxey, G. Rowe, L. Rowe. Middle row: F. Birkin, A.F. Searson, ? Fletcher, L. Topham, -?-, B. Topham, Joe Egglestone, Sam Henshaw, John Brough.

Mr Parker and his sons Ted and Jack relax in the garden in about 1920. All three were miners at the Denby Pit.

Ralph Lynn

Tom Walls

The Home of Entertainment

See and Hear . . .

The Best British Productions

AT

RIPLEY'S POPULAR CINEMA

THE

HIPPODROME

The All British Sound Cinema,
Supported by the Cream of the World's
Productions.

Winifred Shotter

CARNIVAL WEEK ATTRACTIONS.

ALL BRITISH.

MON., TUES. & WED.	THURS., FRI. & SAT.
Ernie Lotinga	**Gene Gerrard**
IN	IN
Dr. JOSSER, K.C.	**OUT of the BLUE**

Proprietors - J. Marshall & Sons

TELEPHONE 17 RIPLEY.

The Cinema that gives Satisfaction

Sydney Howard

Jack Hulbert

8

An advertisement for the Hippodrome cinema that appeared in the carnival programme of 1932.

Right: The Oxford Hippodrome in Derby Road seen here in about 1914, a year or two after it was built. The Hippodrome was another of the exploits of that enterprising Ripley businessman John Marshall. Built to an unusual design by George Wesley Bird, who later became the town surveyor, it seated nearly 400 people and showed a mixture of film and live variety performances. In 1921 the cinema was radically enlarged with a new auditorium behind and at right angles to the first one. The old auditorium was retained and the upper part converted into a dance hall with the old entrance a sweet shop for the cinema. The new theatre could seat over 900 people.

Below: The proscenium stage and balconies of the new Hippodrome. The interior was elaborately decorated and a seven-piece orchestra accompanied the films until the 'talkies' arrived here in 1930. The Marshall family sold their interests in the Hippodrome in 1946 but it continued to operate as a cinema right up to 1991 although, following alterations, bingo was introduced in the lower part while films carried on in the balcony. The cinema part now sits empty awaiting its fate but the lower part is used by Tonkers nightclub.

Left: Jim Gration was the first manager of the Hippodrome and is seen here with his wife Edith, daughter of John Marshall, in about 1910. He was killed in the War in 1917 after being awarded the D.C.M. His brother-in-law Richard took over the cinema and managed it for many years.

Below: This house, known as the White House, stood on a site near to the Market Place and was demolished to build the Hippodrome.

Above: During the General Strike of 1926 the Hippodrome gave free concerts to the striking local miners. This picture taken in May of that year by local photographer Randolph Nield shows the enormous queues that gathered to take advantage of these concerts. The policeman keeping an eye on things is thought to be 'Bobby' Moon from Marehay.

Right: A little boy helps gather the season's impressive harvest of vegetable marrows. This photograph was probably taken in George Large's market garden in Nottingham Road Ripley.

Families making their own music or entertaining themselves and others with singing and dancing was a common and everyday occurence —not so today. This is the Revill family from Brook Lane who were all proficient musicians and enjoyed playing regularly together. Seen here in 1931, they are, from left to right: Doris, Edna, Hilda, Donzie and, in the front, Jim with the concertina. Notice their choice of composer, it is apparently intended to be a punning comment on their playing!

A group of Ripley OAPs assembled on Platform 1 of Butterley station awaiting the train that will take them to Manchester for a show, in about 1950.

This extraordinary photograph taken in Chapel Street in about 1900 shows a troupe of dancing bears. It is hard to believe that it was still possible to see such a sight in a Derbyshire street at the turn of the century.

The Victory Hall in Nottingham Road in about 1922. The building actually contained two halls and a cafe and was built in 1920 and run by a group of Ripley businessman for the showing of films, live shows and for dancing. The top floor of the main hall was a billiards room. It was very popular for a number of years but then went into a decline and was bought by the Co-op in 1928, who converted the main hall into a bakery. The café was hired out for receptions and other functions. After the war the Co-op reconverted the main hall into a dairy. The smaller hall on the left was used for dances and other events up to the 1980s. When the building was eventually demolished flats were built on the site. Note that this view was taken before the construction of Broadway, which is now on the right side of the road beyond the hall.

Opposite above: In the 1940s and 50s the Butterley Pantomimes were a popular entertainment put on by the Company's staff. This glamorous line-up of 1949 consists of, from left to right: Eileen Rickers, Monica Smith, Lilian Watson, Elena Smith, Bernice Bond and ? Bond. The shows were professional affairs, with choreography by Lilian Watson, sets painted by Ann Newman (wife of the General Manager), lighting by Frank Mancy and music by (among others), Alf Woods (violin) and George Thompson (piano).

Opposite below: Another Butterley show, this time *Babes in the Wood*, in the 1950s. After performances in the staff canteen for the Butterley employees, the pantomimes went on tour, with annual shows at the Matlock Pavilion, South Wingfield village hall and Matthew Holland at Selston. The performers are; from left to right: -?-, Iris Frith, Les Leam, Margaret ?, -?-, Charlie Cuttle (producer), -?-, Lilian Watson, Monica Smith, -?-, -?-, Len Rhodes, -?-, ? Rickers.

Left: The mid-1920s were times of austerity for many families in industrial areas like Ripley. Unemployment and national strikes meant that money was short and a family holiday was out of the question. It was during this time that Fred Taylor of Wood Street Methodist Church began to organise summer boy's camps. The first camp in 1926 was a local one at Heage but after that all trips went to the seaside. Part of the fun was travelling in the back of an open lorry! This trip was to Marske near Redcar in 1936.

Below: This group of boys went on the Wood Street camp to Theddlethorpe on the Lincolnshire coast in 1930. The all in cost of a camp was six shillings. The camps have become an institution and still run every year. Since 1947 Ellis Redfern has organised every trip (except for a break during the war years) and after girls were allowed to join the camps in 1955, his wife, Alleyne, has not missed one!

Wood Street boys peeling the spuds for dinner at a summer camp in Lincolnshire in the mid-1930s.

Girls and boys from Wood Street at camp in 1960 at Burnham on Sea.

The Ripley Junior Excelsior Band in about1937. This well-drilled band travelled near and far to compete in competitions of brass band music. The band was founded and trained by Isaac Murfin and the members wore a uniform of gold satin blouses with green trousers, skirts and berets and white gloves. In this picture are the following; front row, left to right: Isaac Murfin, jnr, David Wilkinson, 'Pip' Bonser, -?-, Alwyn Melrose, Winifred Ottewell (mascot), ? Bradley, Derek Foulkes, Dennis Eyre, Les Rogers. Second row: Keith Staley, Iris Ottewell, Edith Burgin, Oliver Wilders, Dennis Leah, Alma Lynam, Harry Melrose (drum major), Mavis Bridges, Mavis Smith, Barbara Joel, Nora Ball, Ursula Clark. Third row: Isaac Murfin, ? Strange, Madge Ford, ? Smith, -?-, ? Ottewell, Cliff Smith, Tom Murfin, Cliff Matthews, Roy College, Mr Ottewell. Fourth row: -?-, -?-, Gwen Fletcher, Kathleen Staley, Marjorie Strange, Connie Frost, Violet Walker, ? Walker, ? Ablott, Jean Barrett.

The home of the Fletcher family in Nottingham Road seen here in about 1910 but better known to most for its later role as the Miners' Welfare. After the Fletchers left it became a school for a short period but, in about 1920, it was acquired as the social centre for local miners and their families. Among other activities there were bowling and football teams. In 1956, encouraged by the popularity of the new Regal ballroom managed by Harry Greatorex, the 'Welfare' started regular ballroom nights and for almost a couple of decades provided a venue for dances and local pop groups. Harry Greatorex ran this too for a time under the name of 'Sunset Boulevard'. The site is now part of Zycomm mobile radio.

Mr Fletcher with his daughter outside their house in Nottingham Road in about 1910.

Mr and Mrs Seal in the garden at Crossley Street in the 1890s.

A production of *Showboat* by Ripley Co-operative Operatic Society on stage at the Hippodrome in 1968. In the cast were; from the left, standing: J. Pickup, Les Land, Stanley Stafford, Jean Bridges, Ken Thompson, Alan Brentnall, Jean Millar and seated, Pauline Elliott and Helen Lathwell.

Rose Cottage in Steam Mill Lane stood opposite the windmill. Standing outside the cottage are Ethell Loades, wife of Herbert Loades the baker, and Lorna Bayliss. The time is the late 1920s.

During the 1960s, pop concerts were organised by Ripley Round Table and held in a marquee in Mr Melrose's grounds at the bottom of Butterley Hill. This one in 1964 featured singer Dave Berry whose recording of 'The Crying Game' was a hit in that year.

Six

Ripley Cottage Hospital

Christmas at Ripley Hospital. A group of staff outside the hospital before taking gifts and Christmas fare to the patients. The man on the right is Dr Thompson and the lady on the right is the matron who, like several matrons in the early days of the hospital, kept a dog which was allowed to roam the wards. This photograph is from the early 1920s.

The decision to build a hospital in Ripley was a very popular one and a grand procession to the stone-laying ceremony was one of the biggest ever seen in Ripley. This photograph, taken by John Marshall from the White House in High Street, shows a big parade coming down Oxford Street in about 1912 that may be a record of this event. If it is not then no matter, this is probably much the way it must have looked!

The laying of the foundation stones at the site of the new hospital in April 1912. Mr F.N. Smith, coalowner, does the job with due pomp and seriousness after an announcement that he had just donated £5 to the fund. In his speech he made reference to the 'deal of trouble they were in' at that time, a reference to a miners' strike that it appears had been on for the last month. He hoped that the miners would take notice of the day's events and say to themselves, 'this hospital is being built not for the rich, but it is built for us miners...the rich and middle classes are not all as bad as some of our leaders make us believe'. Perish the thought that a coalowner's philanthropy should go unappreciated!

The first staff to work at the hospital when it opened.

Councillor B.J.F. Crossley (left) was the president of the hospital fundraising organising committee. Mr Argile (on the right) was the hospital architect.

The hospital opening ceremony on 7 September 1912. The opening was conducted by Mr Charles Ford, a local colliery owner, who had previously donated a horse-drawn ambulance for the use of the town. The hospital movement had been set up only twenty months earlier following a particularly tragic incident that had fired local people into action. A miner injured in an accident at the Pentrich Colliery was taken to Derby by road and was so debilitated by the journey that he died before treatment could be given. A letter to the local paper from the colliery manager, pointing out that local hospital provision may have saved his life, led to a public meeting and the successful campaign to build one. The present League of Friends of the Ripley Hospital continues to raise substantial funds that help to ensure that Ripley will resist the national trend to close small hospitals.

Seven

Trade and Industry

This area has mined coal for centuries but the Butterley Company, established in the late eighteenth century, was responsible for organising large scale mining in and around Ripley. This is Britain Colliery which was beyond Butterley Hall by the Coach Road and close to what is now the Midland Railway Centre. This pit opened in 1848 and closed in 1946. A railway track connected it, and the Butterley works, to Ripley Pit via the so-called Iron Bridge across Nottingham Road.

Smedley's soft drinks factory in Nottingham Road in about 1900. All members of this group are Smedleys, from left to right: Ernold, Ivy, Sally, John, Mary, Percy, Harold and William (father and proprietor).

The matchbox design used by the Ripley match manufacturers Albert and Herbert Loades for the matches produced in their little factory in Steam Mill Lane. The company, set up in 1926, struggled to find a large enough market for their matches until the Ripley Co-op decided to stock them and then the factory's fortunes looked up. It was short-lived, for a fire destroyed everything in 1929.

Above: Ripley Pit in the early years of the century. This pit was the closest to the centre of Ripley and stood on what is now green reclaimed land between Peasehill Road and Colliery Road. It opened in 1863 and merged with Denby Hall in 1949 after which all working was done from Denby and the headstocks were dismantled.

Right: A tall chimney was felled at Ripley Pit in 1907. It is hard to believe now but until the late 1940s Ripley was dominated by the coal mines within and around it. The sights, sounds and smells of coalmining in the area now remain only in people's memories.

These are the celebrated 'Gleben Miners' photographed in 1874 after their unsuccessful attempt to initiate a miners' union in the Ripley pits. The Butterley Company sacked all eleven of them but because of their local standing in the community as 'respected men' their protest attracted wide attention and contributed to the eventual acceptance of union rights in the pits. They are (standing), left to right: S. Shooter, G. Brown, S. Cox, G. Taylor, T. Vickers, J. Stratton. Seated: J. Seal, W. Purdy, T. Wheeldon, J. Wright, T. Purdy.

This is the Miners' Strike Committee of 1926, photographed outside Ripley Hospital. There was great local hardship in the area for miners' families and unrest in the streets was common. London police were drafted in to 'keep the peace' and the Hippodrome gave free concerts for the miners. One of the strike leaders was Oliver Wright, son of J. Wright, in the photograph of the 1874 protesters above.

Above: Miners at Denby Hall Colliery in the 1930s. The miner in the centre is 'Rada' Gale from Codnor and the man on the extreme left is Arthur Ellicott.

Right: Fitters at Ormonde Colliery in about 1952. The man at front left is Lesley Staley.

Above: A group of fitters at Ford's Pit in 1946. Ford's was a disused shaft west of Marehay that was to be reopened and used as a pumping station to clear water from mines in the area. The men are, from left to right: an unknown deputy from Denby, Harry Parkin, Ernie Hallsworth, Bill Eyre, ? Walker, Keith Staley (holding a spanner), Eric Green and Ernest Hall. Keith Staley was fourteen when he started this job.

Left: This is the new headstock, built by Butterley and erected by the fitters to hold the pump at Ford's Pit. In the post-war years thrift was important, and the pump used was a reconditioned Sulzer salvaged from a scrap-yard in Somercotes.

This view of Ford's Pit shows the finished pump in use. The flow pipe is being changed and the pump lifted up the shaft after rain.

Coal-picking at High Holborn, Codnor Gate in about 1906.

Agricultural elevators manufactured by G.C. Ogle were a familiar sight in Ripley at one time. This advertisement appeared in a publication of 1949 when the staff was said to be only just 'building up again after the war' and yet 200 people worked there. Some people still remember that it was common to see a long line of these elevators in Victoria Road waiting to be towed down to the railway station for dispatch.

Mr G.C. Ogle began business as a blacksmith in 1870 in an old chapel at the bottom end of Church Street. In 1903 he moved the firm, by now an expanding agricultural engineering business, to larger premises in the centre of town, the site now occupied by the new council offices in Cromford Road. The firm, at the new premises, produced small engines, boilers and a variety of agricultural equipment including hay, corn and straw elevators, manure distributors, dairying equipment and rollers. This photograph of the staff in about 1905 includes Mr Ogle on the extreme right. He was reputed to have been a good employer but also, like many a shrewd businessman, kept a keen eye on his costs. A story told by the longest serving member of his staff, John Hardstaff (third from right, middle row), confirms this well. Mr Hardstaff was once sent by Mr Ogle to Mansfield to service some dairying equipment and travelled there by bus, his fare paid by the firm. During the day a fog came down and as the buses were cancelled he walked home to Pentrich. On arrival at work at 6.30am the following morning Mr Ogle asked him how he had faired and on hearing of his long walk home said, 'Oh, so you won't be needing the tuppence for the bus then'!

The roller workshop at G.C. Ogle's in the 1940s. All kinds of agricultural rollers were made, including Cambridge and grass rolllers. The goods were all cast and machined from raw materials, cast iron, pig iron and timber, in the company workshops.

The retirement party for a man who had seen almost the complete history of the Ogle company. In 1958 John Hardstaff, who also appears in the staff picture of 1905 (see previous page), retired after sixty years with the firm. He finally retired at seventy-five and the party was held at the King Alfred Hotel in Alfreton. In the photograph, from left to right are: Harry Vallance, Humphrey Ogle, W. Bonsall, -?-, John Hardstaff, Mrs Hardstaff (sitting on the chair that was his leaving gift), Mrs J. Ogle, Ben Marshall, Jack Ogle (managing director).

The branch managers and officials of the Ripley Co-operative Society on a visit to the C.W.S. factories at Lowestoft in 1948.

Making a wheel at Hill's blacksmiths in the early 1920s. Ted Hill was popular with Ripley children and a group of them often gathered to watch him work at his forge which was at the junction of Nottingham Road and Alfred Street. An apprentice, Bob Allsop, worked as a blacksmith with the Co-op at their stables in Crossley Street until the 1960s, and is credited as being the last working blacksmith in the town.

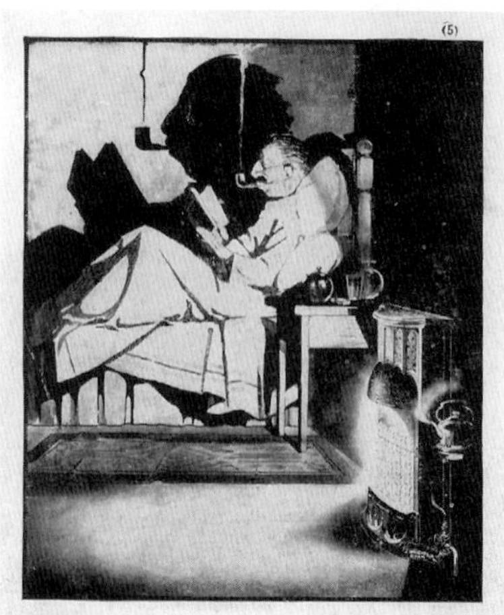

An advertising postcard for the Ripley Gas Company.

Ripley gasworks in Peasehill Road in the 1930s. The old Ripley Pit stood just behind the works and the chimney that shows above the gasholder is probably one of the colliery chimneys. The Ripley Gas Company closed in about 1941 after about one hundred years of gas production. Three generations of the Hatfield family were employed there as managers. Most of the buildings in this view are now gone; only the large building on the left, the retort house which was used for carbonising the coal before gas extraction, remains and is used as a store by the Army Surplus company. Part of the process for purifying the gas was to pass it through a black powdery substance known in the works as 'oxide'. This material extracted sulphur and after a period of use was placed in large boxes in the yard awaiting collection by a chemical company. This substance was rumoured to have useful properties for chest complaints and mothers of children with coughs and colds would bring their offspring to play in the dust!

Above: Blount's ices were said to be the 'whitest' ices in town – they were also very popular! Mr Blount was photographed outside his house in Wall Street with daughter Alice in the cart which was made for them by G.C. Ogle.

Right: Towlson's Mill in Hammersmith made wire before the war and afterwards became Merrill's spring factory. The chimney, which was 200 feet high and a local landmark, was demolished in about 1979.

Above: A view across the fields to Butterley from Pentrich probably photographed in the 1930s. The distant works are Butterley ironworks and the buildings on the right, marked by the tall chimney, are those of Towlson's Mill, Hammersmith.

Left: In Heage Road in the 1940s were flax mills operated by the British Hemp and Flax Development Company. The factory covered about twelve acres and employed 150 people. Flax was collected from growing areas in Derbyshire, Nottinghamshire, Leicestershire and Rutland which was then converted into high quality fibres for linen and a variety of other experimental products. The development of synthetic fibres, however, eventually led to a decline in this trade.

A Butterley bridge erection gang working on a bridge in Tickhill, Yorkshire in about 1905. The men are, from the left: George Fountain, Bert Phillips (behind), Harry Jackson (front), George Amott, the next man, sitting up, is not known, George Allsop (front), Billy Dove and Joe Dove (above). The Butterley Ironworks was founded in 1792 following on two years after the formation of the Butterley Company by Benjamin Outram, William Jessop, Francis Beresford and John Wright. Bridge-building became a major activity and the company was responsible for the construction of many important structures all over the World, including the Sydney harbour bridge and the great span of St Pancras Station in 1868.

A Butterley gang after the erection of a bridge in West Wycombe, Buckinghamshire, in about 1905. During World War II, Butterley works was in great demand for ironwork for Bailey bridges, keels for frigates, tank tracks and harbour pontoons.

The Butterley works 'back yard' photographed, probably in the 1930s, with rows of cast iron pipes waiting to be loaded onto the company's own railway waggons in the background.

A fleet of tank trucks made at Butterley for ICI at Widnes wait in the siding by the Butterley signal box in the 1950s.

(Left) A group of Butterley workers from the early 1900s. The bowler hat denotes 'foreman', and (right) a group of workers from the Butterley pattern shop in about 1922. On the left is Percy Cooke and on the right, Fred Cheetham.

Rivetters making iron pit tubs at the Butterley Codnor Park site in 1952. This part of the Codnor Park site closed in 1965.

One of the many Butterley locos built at the works and used solely for transporting materials such as coal, slag and iron on Butterley's own railway. This engine was Butterley loco no.14, built in 1915. These engines were not used on British Railways track and often failed to comply with their standard design and safety requirements. This engine had special wide buffers for shunting slag.

Butterley Company took the decision to became involved in railways in 1832 after concern, shared by other local coal owners, that canal charges had become prohibitive and the way forward was for independent transport. They formed, with others, the Midland Counties Railway which later became part of the Midland Railway. Many locos were built, but not successfully, for sale to other companies. The waggon works at Codnor Park, however, was more successful and built thousands of waggons to order and, also, as above, for its own use.

Butterley Loco no.6, photographed near a crossing-gate in the Bridge Yard in about 1930 with, from the left: Tom Birkin, snr (driver), Jack Wilmot, in front (driver), Frank Cox (weighman) and Billy Botham (driver). The man standing in the middle is not known. The loco was built before 1898 and scrapped in 1948.

A meeting of directors and officials at the Butterley brickworks at Waingroves in 1967. Among those in the photograph are: third from left, Jack Clark (director), facing him, Cyril Clark (assistant secretary), behind him at the back, John Wright (director). Fourth from right, Percy Elliott (company secretary), on his left, Mr Stanway and on extreme right, Ron Robinson (financial director). Brick-making had been part of the company's activities since at least the middle of the last century. Butterley Brick became an independent company in 1969.

Eight

Carnivals and Special Events

Britannia rules the waves! Part of a Victory Day parade through the centre of Ripley in 1919.

Above: Lord John Sanger's Circus parades along Oxford Street in about 1912. Don't miss the man on stilts! The circus was held on the field by the Horse and Jockey Inn. The pub on the right was called the Horse and Groom.

Left: Massive bonfires were a popular way of celebrating the Coronation of King Edward VII in 1902. This huge pile of combustibles was Codnor's contribution to the rejoicing. It consisted of 2,550 sleepers, 100 tons of timber, 200 gallons of tar, 80 gallons of oil and 200 gallons of paraffin. It was 62 feet high and 36 feet across the base.

Animals of Lord John Sanger's circus in Oxford Street in about 1912. As well as the elephants there are camels and black and white ponies in the parade. The building at the end of Oxford Street on Park Corner, now Bark and Bite, used to be the Co-op café. There is a good view of the shops opposite: the premises on the left belonged to a hairdresser, the next shop, now White's, the jewellers, was a hat shop and the next one, with a blind, belonged to Mr Hogg, the butcher. Further down is another shop with a blind which is now a greengrocer and florist but at the time of the photograph was a fish-and-chip shop. The elephants are reputed to have trumpeted each time they passed the Ripley Zoo entrance in Oxford Street!

A large parade of soldiers in Ripley Market Place during the First World War. It may have been part of a recruiting campaign but as it appears to have involved refreshments, there are ladies laying tables by the town hall, it might have been an event of a more social kind.

This gathering of soldiers outside the Hippodrome may have been part of the victory celebrations at the end of the War or perhaps it was a free concert for those on leave or billeted in Ripley.

A May Day parade in Oxford Street in about 1910.

Celebrating crowds in Codnor on Victory Day in 1919. These families gathered to watch the parade on the corner of Mill Lane and Wright Street by the Lord Byron and Miners Arms.

The Whit Monday Sunday School walks to the Codnor Monument were a big event in the calendar for families in Ripley and Codnor. This group of children in their new white dresses and suits were from the Ebenezer Church Sunday School in 1909. The little girl in the middle with the flowers is Winnie Kemp from Ripley.

The Ripley Area Home Guard in a group photograph from 1940. Ripley people will recognise many of these faces; amongst them are, second row, tenth from the right: W.I.Pickard (grandfather of Tony Pickard, tennis player), on his left, Bernard Bradley (Legal Executive with Ellis-Fermor and Negus for 50 years) and on his left Wilf Marshall (Marshall's Ironmongers and son of John Marshall, founder of the Hippodrome, etc.). In the same row, second and third from right are Jack and Charles Mason (Oxford Street outfitters) and in the third row, second from right, Herbert Atkins (solicitor).

Poppy sellers outside the Town Hall in about 1926. The British Legion began in 1925 and this is one of their early appeals in Ripley. The tall lady in the centre is Mrs M.E. Head.

In 1960 The Campaign for Nuclear Disarmament staged a march from London to Holy Loch in Scotland as a protest against Polaris nuclear submarine bases. The Ripley branch of CND joined the procession as it passed through Ripley and down Nottingham Road.

A street party in Stirland Street, Codnor to celebrate the Queen's Siver Jubilee in 1977. George Eyre, news photographer, is at the back on the left.

Above: Church processions to the Market Place in about 1925. As representatives of each church arrived their banners were placed together to one side while the services took place. Children had separate services at the other end.

Left: The first Ripley Carnival took place in 1932. It was an elaborately planned affair with many events taking place over four days and ending with a big procession. This is from the brightly coloured cover of the first carnival magazine – *The Rip*.

Above: This carnival had a King and Queen and a 'celebrity' visitor. The King was played by Bert Weekly and the Queen by Nancy Marshall and the celebrity was announced to be Miss Wyn Richmond the film star (right). After the carnival was over it became known that her visit was in fact a hoax, the lady was a hairdresser from Nottingham.

Right: Members of the 1932 Carnival Committee were depicted in *The Rip* in this caricature style. W.W.Shephard, solicitor, of Ellis-Fermor and Shephard was editor of the magazine.

Travel by
LONDON, MIDLAND & SCOTTISH RAILWAY.

SPECIAL TRAINS

Will be run to the Carnival from Derby and Intermediate Stations, as under:—

WEDNESDAY
(24th August) Leave Derby ... **5.0** p.m.
Ripley Carnival Royal Special.

THURSDAY
(25th August) Leave Derby ... **6.30** p.m.

FRIDAY
(26th August) Leave Derby ... **2.0** p.m.
Ripley Carnival Royal Ox-Roasting Special.

SATURDAY
(27th August) Leave Derby ... **1.30** p.m.

TRAINS will Leave RIPLEY EACH DAY at 10.30 p.m.

FARES:

DERBY ... ... **1/6** Return
LITTLE EATON & COXBENCH **1/2** Return
KILBURN ... ... **6d.** Return
DENBY ... ... **4d.** Return

The 1932 Carnival had such a high profile that special trains were laid on for visitors from all around the area.

Ripley Scouts joined the carnival procession turned out like a scene from *King Kong*.

A group of carnival characters in fancy dress for the 1934 revels. This group was responsible for the carnival magazine. In the group are; second from left, Mrs Shephard and sitting, left to right: Mr Lear, 'Monkey' Jackson and Charlie Small.

Above: *The Rip* sellers for the 1932 Carnival assembled for a photograph by Randolph Nield before they terrorise the crowd. In the centre is Bert Weekly (Carnival King), to his right, Nancy Marshall (Carnival Queen) and to his left, W.W. Shephard and Mrs Shephard.

Left: A 1932 *Carnival Magazine* caricature of Mr W.E. Masterson, chairman of the Magazine Committee.

Nine

Out of Town

A view down the bridle path from Sandham Lane to Street Lane in the 1930s. This pretty walk was a favourite route for couples on summer evenings. Unfortunately, it is now overgrown and no longer the romantic walk that it was.

Above: Haymaking on a small-holding in Peasehill in 1926.

Left: The Cromford Canal at Lower Hartshay in about 1910. In very cold winters the canal froze over and some energetic characters would skate all the way to Cromford.

The view from Hartshay Hill in the 1930s.

The Ripley Show was revived in 1945 after a lapse of about twenty years. During the war years the Ripley Allotment Holders Association and the Dig for Victory Committee had joined forces to encourage gardening and food production and after the war turned their efforts to peacetime pride in food production. This photograph was probably taken at the 1948 show.

The centre of Pentrich and the church in about 1934. The Victorian lamp and signpost were later badly damaged by a lorry and never fully repaired. Although Pentrich appears now to be a peaceful country backwater it has not always been so. Pentrich was once the senior member of the administrative partnership with Ripley and they shared one church until All Saint's was built in Ripley in 1821. Ripley grew faster than Pentrich as industry brought work and wealth to the area but many felt exploited and when a group of disenchanted workers from Pentrich rose against their employers they were harshly put down. The 'Pentrich Revolution' gained national attention and Shelley was moved to write about the injustices of their trial. The man with the bicycle in this photograph is Mr Len Wood, Ripley's best-known photographer and collector of photographs of the area.

The Cromford Canal at Hartshay in about 1910. Just visible in the centre of the picture is a narrow boat being pulled by a horse on the towpath to the left.

This view of Pentrich across the fields from Asher Lane in about 1950 does not at first look very different from the view today but closer study reveals the changes. The church, top right, is totally obscured by trees in this view.

The post office in Pentrich in about 1910 with the postmaster's family standing in the garden.

The Wayside Cafe, Pentrich in about 1950. This easily recognised house at the top of Asher Lane in the centre of the village was once the post office (above) and was run as a summer café for walkers and cyclists during the 1940s and '50s. The house is in two parts and the right-hand one was the café, or rather the garden was, for visitors sat on the grass, or one of those long benches, to drink their tea and eat seed cake.

This delightful photograph taken in 1902 shows the Birks family in the stackyard of The Homestead in Butterley Fields. The farm was on the outskirts of Ripley by Bridle Lane off Lowes Hill, where a new development called The Spinney now is. As Samuel Birks is wearing his suit and a bowler hat in this photograph it is unlikely that he has been raking as much hay as his offspring have, but then the wearing of a bowler hat at this time usually indicated the status of 'foreman'! The family were as follows, from left to right: William (Edmund), Jane, Hetty, Frederick, Sam, Elizabeth, Ellen and Samuel. The men all had jobs at the Butterley Company as well as working on the farm.

Above: St Matthew's church, Pentrich in about 1912. Built in the twelfth century with fifteenth century alterations the church has recently acquired a new bell-frame which will permit bell-ringing to recommence after a break of about forty years.

Left: The interior of St Matthew's church in about 1912.

Ten

Schooldays

The children of the Buxton family outside their home in Heage Road in 1912. They are, from left to right: George, Gladys, Doris, Carrie, Eva and Charles. Mrs Buxton ran the post office in Heage Road and later a sewing machine shop in Oxford Street. Doris was one of the first telephone operators at the exchange in Ripley, initially in Nottingham Road and later in Moseley Street.

The boys of a primary class at the Ripley Council Schools in Shirley Road in about 1912.

The Council Schools in Shirley Road, facing onto Crossley Park. The site is now part of an estate of new houses.

Above: The playground and inner buildings of the Council Schools in about 1920.

Right: Mrs Adelaide Large, schoolteacher at Jessop Street, Codnor and later at Waingroves School, in about 1920. She lived in Nottingham Road, close to the Iron Bridge, where her husband ran a market garden.

The girls of a primary class at the Ripley Council Schools in Shirley Road in 1926. They are; back row, left to right: Ida Brown, Alma Hardy, Joyce Gasgoine, Ruth Statham, Ada Cutts, Violet Jackson, Ada Riley, Ada Haynes, Grace Whooley, Marion Cope, Gladys Birks. Third row: Joan Hardstaff, Hilda Staley, Elsie Travers, Violet Watson, Vera Lenny, Hilda Brookhouse, Alice Lacey, Frances Clay, Marion Thorpe, Frances Severn, Mavis Disney, ? Hardstaff. Second row: Joyce Peale, Gladys Langley, Joyce Norman, Louie West, ? Jackson, Elsie Lynam, Joyce Revel, Dorothy Gregory, Alice Hayllgrove, Lily Russell, Violet Haynes. Front row: Kathy Aldred, Adelaide Wilders, Nora Day, Eva Hardy, Mary Davell, ? Brown, Kitty Redfern, Olive Cresswell, Olive Cutts, Margaret Statham, Cora Gasgoine.

Headmaster, Mr Yeomans, with the last pupils of Lower Hartshay school before it closed in the 1970s.

ve: The quadrangle of the Ripley
ıncil Schools in 1924.

:t: Bert Rogerson (also known as
go') taught handicrafts at Ripley
ıncil Schools for over thirty years.
also ran adult classes and taught
liers who were billeted in Ripley
ing the last war. He was well
wn around the town for his craft
s and was often consulted for
ice on problems of construction.
ring the building of the
podrome he gave advice on the
gn of the balcony supports. He
an teaching in 1914 and retired
952 having taught in the same
sroom from beginning to end.

Above: Children from St John's School, Ripley on visit to the Houses of Parliament with their MP, M Oliver, in 1948.

Left: Members of a large family. Miner George Jackson, who lived in Brook Lane, had a family of sixteen children. He is seen here with Percy and George while a few more of them appear as faces a the window.